While I'm Still Here
Endangered Animals Speak Out

Written and illustrated by
Jodie A Cooper

Every animal featured in this book is on the endangered spectrum.

My hope in creating this book is for these magnificent creatures to remain in the wild for many future generations. If we teach our children how to respect and be harmonious with all living beings on Earth, a better future for everyone will result. Each of us can make a positive impact, one ripple at a time.

Dedication

This book is dedicated to Mini Cooper. You inspire me every day to be a better person and create a better world for you to live in. I love you to the moon and back.

I am an African Elephant. You can find me throughout the savannas of sub-Saharan Africa. I am a habitat modifier, beneficially changing the ecosystem around me. This supports not only elephants but other species. I eat plants, leaves, fruit, and bark, up to 440 lbs a day. I must have water to survive. I live in a female-led herd. I am a majestic animal, the largest mammal on land. I can live up to 70 years, grow to be up to 13 feet tall and 24 feet long, and weigh up to 13,000 pounds. Did you know I flap my large ears to keep me cool? My trunk is used not only to reach food but helps me communicate. Climate change causing drought and land development destroy my habitat. Poachers sell my tusks in the ivory trade. I am hunted for big game thrill. I am captured and forced to perform in circuses and for rides. **Please leave me be while I'm still here.**

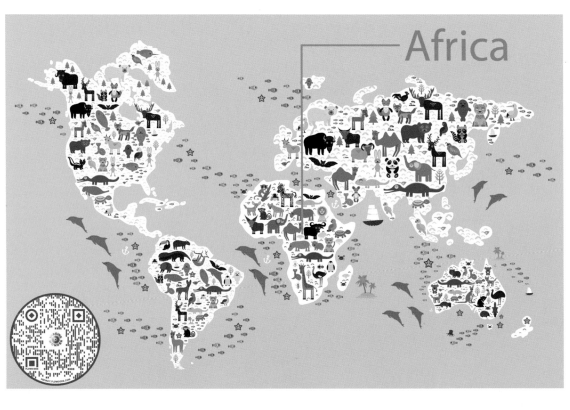

Africa

I am a Mountain Gorilla living on the volcanic slopes of Uganda, Rwanda, and the Congo. I am a social animal and travel in a pack of 5 to 30 gorillas, led by a dominant, older male called a "silverback." I am very intelligent and can be taught sign language. I can live up to 35 years, grow up to 6 feet in height and weigh up to 480 pounds. Females are about one half the size of males. I am one of the largest primates and have thicker fur than other gorillas. I can climb, but you'll usually find me on the ground. I spend 5 hours a day eating roots, fruit, and tree bark. Did you know I can stand up and walk on my back legs? Every gorilla has a distinct nose print. I have a fierce voice that I use when I am threatened. Farming and forest production destroy my habitat. Climate change, human diseases, and traps are a threat to me. I am hunted for sales to zoos and collecting my head and hands for trophies. **Please leave me be while I'm still here.**

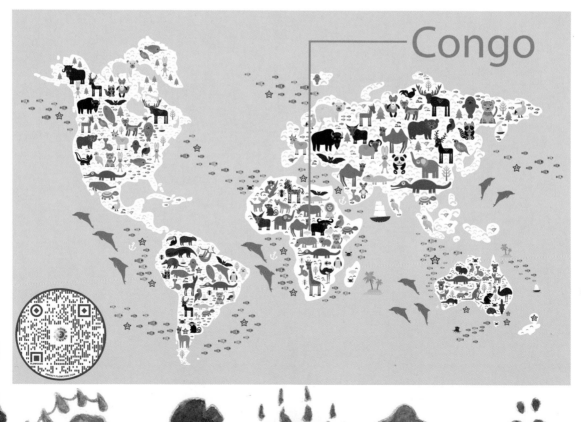

Congo

I am an African Lion, called the "King of the Jungle." I am found in sub-Saharan Africa. I am social and live in a pride of typically three males, twelve females, and cubs. I can live up to 14 years, grow to be 6 feet long, weigh up to 420 pounds, with a tail of up to 40 inches in length! Lions are the only cat species where males and females each have a distinct look. Males have a beautiful head of hair extended down the neck and chest called a mane. Lionesses in the group are all related and are cooperative hunters, most often at dawn or dusk. They can roam up to 100 miles a day, hunting larger animals. When not hunting, lions sleep. Male lions will protect the females in the pride, but the females protect the cubs. My primary threat is from humans who encroach my habitat for farmland, poison, or kill me to keep me away from themselves or their livestock. I am hunted as a trophy animal and by poachers who sell my body parts in illegal trade. **Please leave me be while I'm still here.**

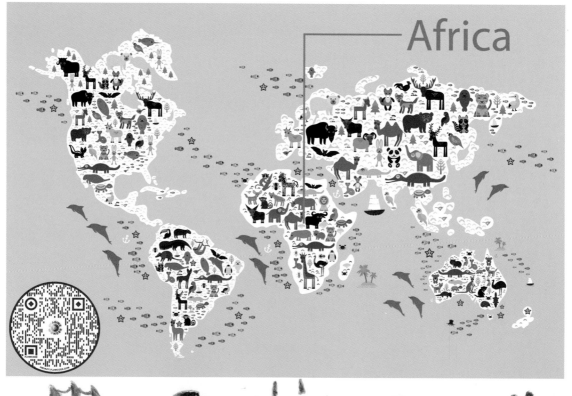

Africa

I am a Black Rhinoceros found in sub-Saharan Africa. Although I am known as a black rhino, I am actually gray. I can live up to 50 years, grow up to 6 feet tall, 12 feet long, and weigh up to 3000 pounds! I am a solitary animal, browsing the lands for food at night, dusk, and dawn. I use my pointed lip to get fruit and leaves from branches of trees and bushes. During the day, you can find me lying in the shade or wallowing in the mud as my hide, though thick, is sensitive to the sun. I will charge when threatened and can run 35 miles per hour! Did you know my two horns can grow up to 5 feet long? I use them for protection and battle. I have great hearing and sense of smell to make up for my poor eyesight. I can be hunted by large cats, but humans are my main predator. I am hunted by poachers solely for my horns, which is sought for use in Eastern medicines and ornamental use in North Africa and the Middle East. **Please leave me be while I'm still here.**

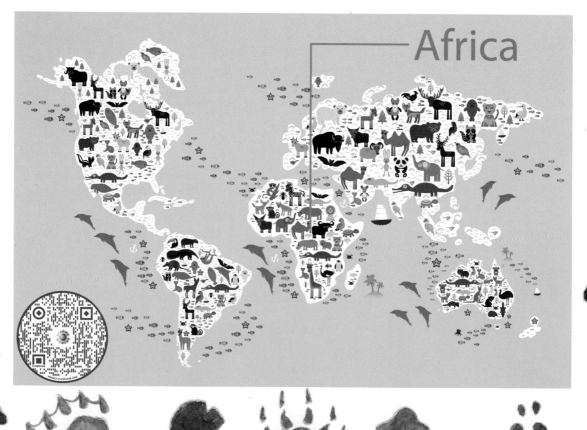

Africa

I am a Giraffe found in dry sub-Saharan Africa. I am social and live in herds of primarily females and calves with a singular male, or just males. I am the tallest mammal in the world, reaching heights of up to 19 feet. My legs alone are taller than the average human. I can live up to 25 years and weigh up to 2800 pounds! I use my 21-inch tongue to pluck food from the treetops. Acacia trees are my favorite. I help pollinate by transferring pollen from one tree to another. I regurgitate my food and chew it as cud. I walk by swinging both legs on the same side, called "pacing." My dinner-plate-sized hooves help me not sink in loose sand. I can gallop up to 35 miles per hour, and a kick from my strong legs can kill or injure another animal. Did you know that I give birth standing up? I am a gentle creature posing no threat to man or animal. My coat has beautiful patterns, and no two of us are alike. I am threatened by habitat loss, deforestation, charcoal production, and disease. I am hunted as a trophy and for international trade of my bones, tail, and hide. **Please leave me be while I'm still here.**

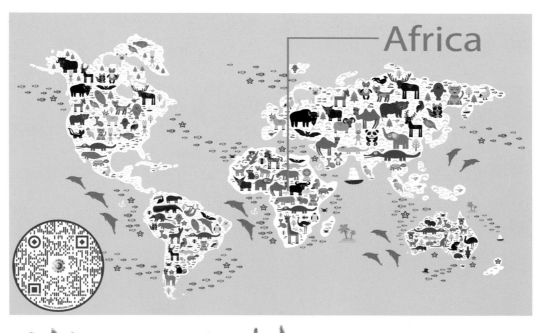

I am a Green Sea Turtle found in tropical and subtropical coastal waters. I am one of the world's largest turtle species weighing up to 700 pounds and growing up to 5 feet in length! I can live up to 80 years. You can tell me apart from other sea turtles because I have a shell called a "carapace" covering my whole body. I also have a single scale in front of my eyes. My flippers move me swiftly through the water. As a youngster, I eat crabs and jellyfish. As an adult, I eat seagrass and algae, which helps fortify the seagrass bed. Did you know that females migrate to lay their eggs, often on the same beaches where they were hatched? I will dig a pit in the sand with my flippers, lay up to 200 eggs, cover the pit and return to the ocean. My eggs are stolen for food, and many hatchlings never make it to the water due to vehicle traffic and beach development. I am threatened by rising sea temperatures and disease. Oceanic pollution and debris disturb me. I get snared in gillnets and shrimp nets and die. I am hunted for meat, leather, and as a trophy. **Please leave me be while I'm still here.**

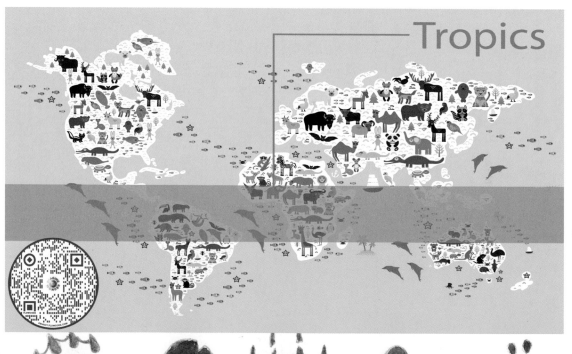

Tropics

I am an Orca, sometimes called a "killer whale." Did you know that I am not a whale at all, rather the largest mammal of the dolphin species? I can be found in every ocean, though I prefer cold coastal and polar waters. I can grow up to 32 feet long and weigh up to 6 tons! I can live up to 60 years. I have a large, dark dorsal fin, a single blowhole, and teeth as long as 4 inches on my top and bottom jaws. I swim in a female-dominant pod of around 40. My pod has distinctive communication that helps us recognize each other, and we hunt cooperatively. I am very intelligent and trainable, which is why I am captured and sold to marine parks. I am a very social animal, and do not thrive in captivity. Because I cannot freely swim and dive, my dorsal fin collapses in captivity. Due to boredom and stress, I develop repetitive behaviors causing harm to myself and others. I am often slaughtered by illegal whaling vessels. **Please leave me be while I'm still here.**

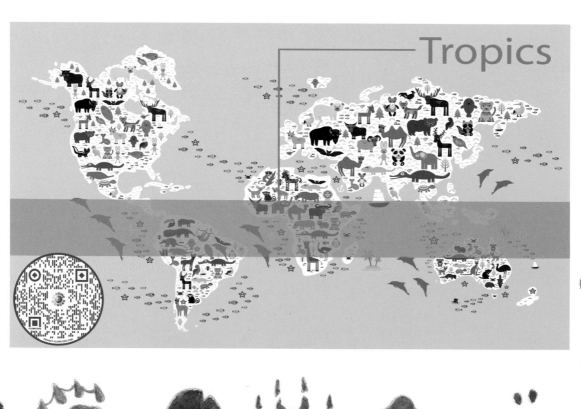

I am a Hippopotamus, called a "river horse" by the Greeks. I am found in sub-Saharan Africa, where I live near rivers, lakes, and mangrove swamps. I can live up to 50 years, grow to be 18 feet in length, and weigh up to 3500 pounds! I spend up to 16 hours each day submerged in water or in the mud to stay cool. Did you know I am a good swimmer, but mostly walk or leap on the bottom of the waterbed? I can hold my breath for 5 minutes! My ears, eyes, and nostrils are high on my head, so I can see and breathe while still being mostly underwater. I feed at night, eating mostly grass and fruits. My calves can nurse while underwater by closing her ears and nostrils. When in the sun, I secrete a substance that moisturizes and protects my skin from the sun. Due to my size, strength, and speed, the only predator for adults is humans. My habitat is threatened by logging and human settlement. I am illegally hunted for the ivory of my teeth, for meat, and for my skin. **Please leave me be while I'm still here.**

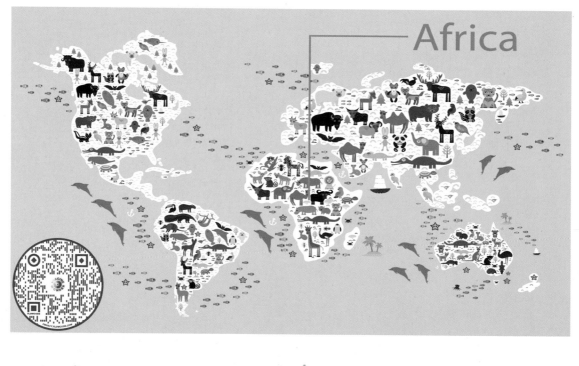

Africa

I am a Magellanic Penguin, named after the explorer who discovered me in the early 1500s. I am found on both the Atlantic and Pacific sides of Southern South America. I am the largest of the warm-weather penguins. I can live up to 20 years, stand about 28 inches tall, and weigh up to 10 pounds. I have very dense, oily feathers that keep me waterproof. Known for my black body and white belly, I blend in with the ocean. My body is built for swimming with webbed feet and long flippers. Did you know that I mate for life and return to the same place I was born to nest? I eat fish, diving up to 300 feet for food. My habitat is threatened by climate change causing heavy rains that flood nesting sites as well as warming waters, depleting plankton supplies. I compete for food sources due to overfishing. Pollution from oil spills remains my greatest threat. **Please leave me be while I'm still here.**

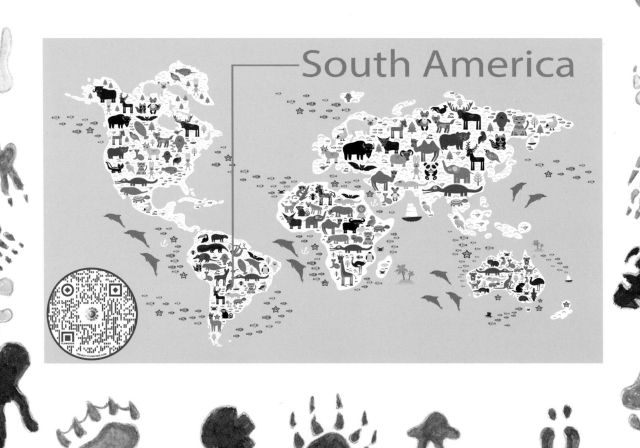

South America

I am a Beluga Whale found in shallow coastal arctic waters. I can live up to 50 years, grow up to 17 feet long, and weigh up to 3500 pounds. I am the smallest of whales, with no dorsal fin and a round head with a prominent forehead called a melon. I live in pods of varying sizes and am very social. I am vocal, called the "canary of the sea" because I can whistle, clang, click, and mimic other sounds. I feed mostly on fish but also eat crustaceans and octopi. I am white in color as an adult, but my calves are born gray or brown and don't turn white until around age 5. During the winter, I will rub my body on the gravel bottoms to shed skin. Did you know I can turn my head in all directions? I am highly intelligent and can be trained to do tricks. I am hunted to be sold to marine parks for entertainment, by commercial fisheries and Indigenous people for meat. Climate change and pollution threaten my habitat. **Please leave me be while I'm still here.**

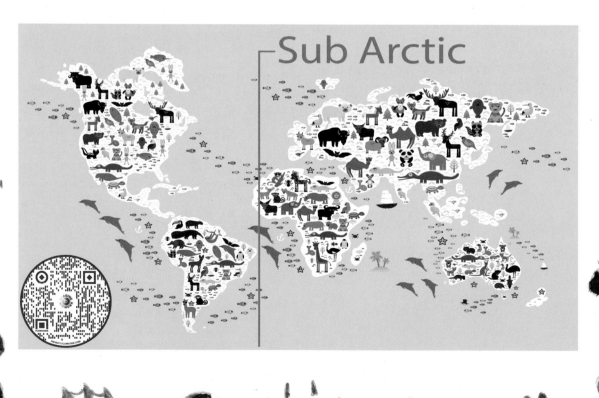

Sub Arctic

I am a Koala. Although I am called a Koala "bear," I am a marsupial with a pouch for raising offspring. You will find me in Eastern and Southeast Australia. I can live up to 18 years, grow to be 30 inches long, and weigh up to 30 pounds. I am a solitary creature. The eucalyptus tree is both food and home for me. I eat up to a pound of eucalyptus leaves a day, getting all the water I need from the leaves. Did you know I have a very slow metabolism, which is why I sleep up to 20 hours a day? I climb and sling to trees with my opposing thumbs, rough pads, and claws. I comb my coarse, wool-like fur with my fused toes. When my baby is born, he is less than 1 inch in size with no fur and closed eyes and ears! He will live in my pouch for about 6 months. Climate change is my greatest threat. Increasing temperatures cause eucalyptus to produce fewer leaves or shed them all to conserve water. Higher levels of carbon dioxide cause eucalyptus trees to produce fewer nutrients. My woodland habitat is shrinking from logging and forest fires. **Please leave me be while I'm still here.**

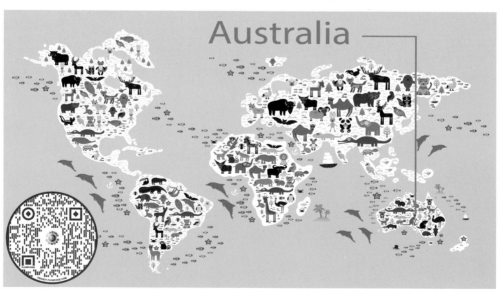

Australia

What a wonderful world it would be
if you could be you and I could be me.
If differences were respected
and peace was accepted,
if we protected our air, sea, and land,
and lent a helping hand,
if we cherished all things living
and had a spirit of giving,
if we used only what we need
and turned our backs on greed,
if we chose love and harmony,
all beings could be free.
What a wonderful world it could be!

What can you do to help save the animals?

Protect your environment
Do not support marine life parks or "swim with" programs
Support environmental protection policies
Use sustainable products such as bamboo
Use eco-friendly cleaning and laundry products
Reuse, reduce, and recycle
Learn about climate change
Use biodegradable single-use items
Continue learning
Support credible wildlife organizations

A portion of the proceeds from this book will be donated to Animal Defenders International

Some credible organizations you can visit:
Animal Defenders International
The Cana Foundation
African Wildlife Fund
Climate Change
One Green Planet
Wildlife Conservation Society

And now it's your turn to get your artist on!

The following pages are line illustrations from this book for you to color.

Some final thoughts

"Will these trophies be all we have left someday; tokens of a wild nature we once knew?"
—Michael Paterniti, National Geographic

"What right do we have to do nothing about it?"
—Shelter to Home, Wyandotte, Michigan, USA

"A true conservationist is a man who knows that the world is not given by his fathers, but borrowed from his children."
—John James Audubon

About the Author

Jodie A Cooper is a lifelong lover of animals and nature. Becoming a Yoga Instructor led her to vegetarianism and enhanced her compassion for all living things. Jodie is committed to education about animal welfare, protecting the environment, and making the world a better place. Always creative, Jodie began painting and writing in recent years. This is her first book. She resides with her husband in Trenton, Michigan.

Visit Jodie at www.JodieACooper.com

Acknowledgments

To Gerry for your unfailing love and support.
To Erika for editing, for being my constant sounding board.
To Keith C. Saylor for your digital mastery.
To Karen Strauss for making my dream a reality.
To Soul Camp Creative for your wisdom and encouragement—

WHOOSH!

Scan the QR code with your phone camera to find more titles like this from Imagine and Wonder

© Copyright 2021, Imagine & Wonder, Publishers, New York
All rights reserved. www.imagineandwonder.com
ISBN: 9781953652867
Library of Congress Control Number: 2021933214

Your guarantee of quality
As publishers, we strive to produce every book to the highest commercial standards. The printing and binding have been planned to ensure a sturdy, attractive publication which should give years of enjoyment.

Replacement assurance
If your copy fails to meet our high standards, please inform us and we will gladly replace it. admin@imagineandwonder.com

Printed in China by Hung Hing Off-set Printing Co. Ltd.

Scan the QR code to find other
amazing adventures and more from
www.ImagineAndWonder.com